Things to Make and Do
for Valentine's Day

# Things to Make and Do for Valentine's Day

## by Tomie de Paola

**SCHOLASTIC INC.**

NEW YORK · TORONTO · LONDON · AUCKLAND · SYDNEY · TOKYO

FOR CELIA

ISBN 0-590-11821-8

Copyright © 1967 by Franklin Watts, Inc. All rights reserved. This edition is published by Scholastic Inc., 730 Broadway, New York, NY 10003, by arrangement with Franklin Watts, Inc.

12 11 10 9 8 7 6 5 4                                    4 5 6 7/8

Printed in the U.S.A.                                    07

February

14

Valentine's Day

On Valentine's Day we tell people
how much we like them.

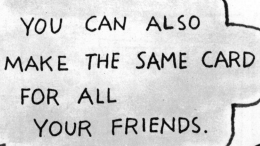

YOU CAN ALSO
MAKE THE SAME CARD
FOR ALL
YOUR FRIENDS.

IT'S EASY
WHEN YOU KNOW
HOW TO MAKE
A PRINT.

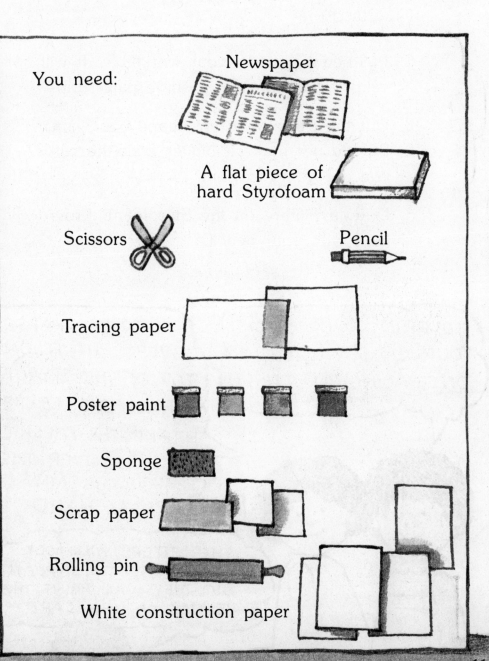

You need:

Newspaper

A flat piece of hard Styrofoam

Scissors

Pencil

Tracing paper

Poster paint

Sponge

Scrap paper

Rolling pin

White construction paper

How to do it:

1. Put newspaper on your worktable. It will keep the table clean if some paint drips.

2. Cut the Styrofoam any shape you want. But do not make it bigger than the cards you are going to print.

3. Draw a picture on the Styrofoam. Press hard with your pencil.

TO PRINT WORDS ON YOUR CARD, WRITE THEM ON TRACING PAPER FIRST.

TURN THE PAPER OVER. PUT IT ON TOP OF THE STYROFOAM TRACE THE LETTERS. TAKE THE PAPER OFF AND GO OVER THE LETTERS AGAIN. PRESS HARD.

THE LETTERS WILL LOOK BACKWARDS ON THE STYROFOAM. BUT THEY WILL PRINT THE RIGHT WAY ON THE CARD.

4. Sponge the paint over the top of your drawing.

5. Try printing on a piece of scrap paper. Put the paper on top of the drawing. Roll over it with a rolling pin.

Not enough paint

Too much paint

Just right

6. Fold or cut the construction paper into cards.

7. Print as many cards as you want. (Each new card needs fresh paint.)

8. Let the cards dry.

YOU CAN PRINT MORE THAN ONE DRAWING ON A CARD.

# If you want, you can make envelopes for the cards.

You need:

Paper that is bigger than your card

Scotch tape

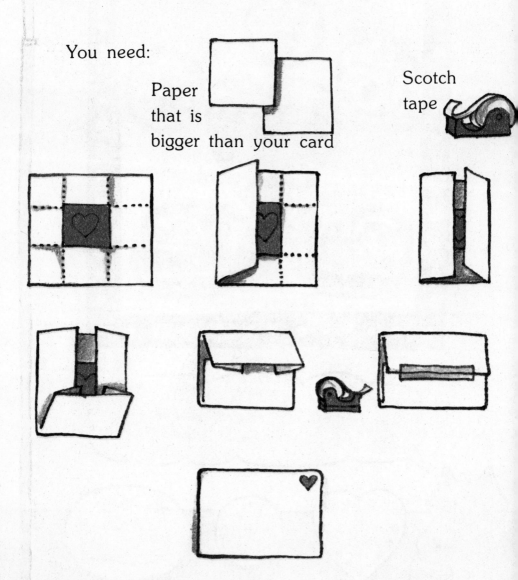

# Valentine Mailbag

You need:

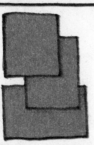

Three pieces of
red construction
paper

Pipe cleaners

Scotch tape

Scissors

Glue

Black crayon

A big
shopping bag

IT'S FUN
TO MAKE A
MAILBAG FOR
YOUR CLASSROOM.

How to do it:

1. Cut out hearts from the red construction paper.

 A big
heart
for a
body.

 A smaller
heart
for a
head.

Two small
hearts
for ears.

 Seven small hearts
for a tail.

Four small hearts
for paws.

2. Glue the ears to the head.

3. Draw eyes, a nose, and a mouth on the head.

Make the mouth
wide so a valentine
can go through it.

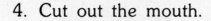

4. Cut out the mouth.

5. Glue or tape the pipe cleaners on like this.

6. Glue the seven small hearts together for a tail.

7. Glue the tail to the back of the body.

8. Glue the paws to the body.

9. Glue the body and face to the front of the bag.

10. At the mouth, cut the bag open.

11. Tape the top of the bag shut.

12. Now hang it up and fill it with valentines.

## Valentine Jokes and Fun

What did the boy octopus say to the girl octopus on Valentine's Day?

I want to hold your hand, hand, hand, hand, hand, hand, hand, hand.

Sal: How can you tell an elephant from a valentine card?

Al: I don't know.

Sal: Then don't get a job with the post office.

What did the valentine card say to the stamp?

Stick with me and we'll go places!

Knock knock.
Who's there?
Olive.
Olive who?
Olive you!

How many hearts can you
find in this picture?

The answer is on the last page.

Here are some valentine tongue twisters. Can you say them five times very fast?

Lila's love laughs loudly.

Sweaty Sam's sweetheart Susie
swears she's sick of Sweaty Sam.
Sweaty Sam says Susie's silly
so he's swell to Sally Ann.

Patty's purple passion Percy
passed his plate for pudding, please.
Patty paused and paled politely,
passing Percy pureed peas.

Vile Violet's varnished valentine vanished.

# You can make fancy sandwiches for the party.

For six people, you need:

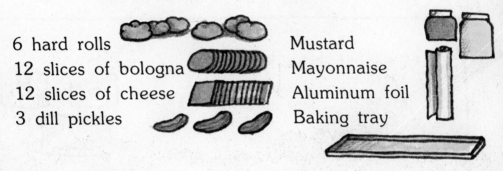

6 hard rolls
12 slices of bologna
12 slices of cheese
3 dill pickles

Mustard
Mayonnaise
Aluminum foil
Baking tray

How to do it:

1. Have your mother set the oven at 350°.

2. Cut each roll in half.

3. Cut the pickles into very thin slices.

4. Put 1 teaspoon of mustard, 3 teaspoons of mayonnaise, 2 slices of bologna, 2 slices of cheese, and 2 slices of pickles on each roll.

5. Wrap each sandwich in aluminum foil. Put on a baking tray.

6. Bake the sandwiches for 20 minutes.

How about a
chocolate snowball valentine
for dessert?

For six people, you need:

2 boxes of frozen strawberries
1 pound cake
1 quart of chocolate ice cream
Marshmallow topping
Shredded coconut
Cookie sheet
Spatula

How to do it:

1. Let the frozen strawberries melt.

2. Cut 6 thin slices of pound cake. Put them on the cookie sheet.

3. Put 2 large spoonfuls of marshmallow topping on each.

4. Have your mother set the oven at 350°. Bake the slices of pound cake for 15 minutes.

5. Take the spatula and put each piece of cake on a plate.

6. Cover each piece of cake with ice cream.

7. Add 3 spoonfuls of melted strawberries.

8. Sprinkle coconut over the top.

# A heart tree looks pretty on the table.

You need:

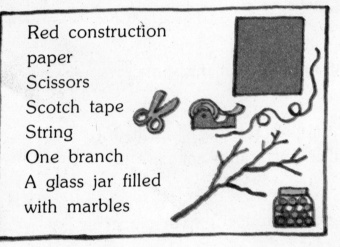

Red construction
paper
Scissors
Scotch tape
String
One branch
A glass jar filled
with marbles

How to do it:

1. Cut out hearts of all different sizes from the red paper.

2. Tape a piece of string to each heart.

3. Tie the hearts to the branch.

4. Stick the branch in the marbles.

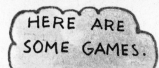

HERE ARE SOME GAMES.

## A Valentine Relay Race

You need:

Red construction paper
Scissors
Black crayon
A piece of string six times
as long as your arm

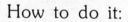

How to do it:

1. Before the party,
   cut out a heart
   for each player.

IF YOU HAVE
AN ODD NUMBER OF PLAYERS
(LIKE 9) MAKE AN
EXTRA HEART.

2. Think of some things to do, such as: jump, crawl, hop, skip, and walk backwards.

3. Take two hearts. Write the same thing to do on each.

4. Do this for all the hearts. Put the hearts into two piles like this.

How to play:

1. Make two teams of players.

2. Put the string on the floor.

3. Line each team up behind it.

4. Put a pile of hearts across
   the room from each team.

5. On "Go" the first player on each team runs up to a pile and takes a heart.

6. The players then come back, doing what it says on the hearts.

7. When the first players get back to their teams, the next players run to the hearts.

8. The team finished first wins.

# The Heartbeat Game

How to play:

1. Sit the players on the floor in a circle.

2. Show the five things they must say and do.

Hit the floor
twice and say,
"Bam, bam."

Cross your arms.
Slap your knees
twice and say,
"Slap, slap."

Clap your hands
twice and say,
"Clap, clap."

Tap your head
twice and say,
"Tap, tap."

Tap your heart
twice and say,
"Beat, beat."

3. Give the
   players a
   chance to
   practice.

4. On "Go" all players must keep doing the five
   things in the right order and saying the right
   words. Any player who misses is out.

# Here's a card trick
# to do at your party.

How to do it:

1. Have a friend mix a deck of cards.

2. Put the cards face down on the table.

3. You cut the deck and hold on to the top half.

4. Ask your friend to look at the top card on the table and remember it.

5. While your friend is doing this, you peek at the bottom card in your hand.

6. Put the cards you are holding on top of the cards on the table.

7. Have your friend cut the deck a few times.

8. Now have your friend deal the cards — one at a time, face up, off the top of the deck.

9. You can tell which card your friend looked at and remembered.

10. It's the one right after the card you peeked at.

# Valentine Presents

YOU CAN MAKE NEAT PRESENTS WITH "BAKER'S CLAY."

You need:

Newspaper
1 cup of flour
½ cup of salt
⅓ cup of water
Cookie sheet
Aluminum foil
A large bowl
Pencil
Poster paints
Shellac
Brushes
Colored string
Scissors

How to do it:

1. Put newspaper on your worktable.

2. Cover the cookie sheet with aluminum foil.

3. Put the flour, salt, and water in the bowl.

4. Mix it with your hands until it feels like clay.

5. Have your mother set the oven at 275°.

6. Put a small lump of the clay on the cookie sheet.

7. Make a shape you like.

8. Do this as many times as you want. But leave room between each shape.

9. Poke a hole in each shape with the pencil.

10. Bake the shapes until they are hard and dry. It takes about an hour.

11. Let them cool on the cookie sheet.

12. Now paint the shapes any way you want.

13. When the paint is dry, shellac each shape. Do one side first. Let it dry before you do the other side.

14. Put a piece of colored string through each hole.

15. Now you have valentine presents to give your friends.

There are 11 hearts
in this picture.